Mommy, Daddy Can I Have? Teaching our children simple money management tips

I0504775

By
Rosalyn Morgan

ACKNOWLEDGEMENT

This book is dedicated to my children, Joe and Rae, and my godchildren Stephon, Ahleena, and Autumn.

I want to give a special thanks to Santanya for her encourage me to write this book and to my daughter, Rae and my goddaughter, Autumn for their God given creative talents on the front and back book cover.

TABLE OF CONTENTS

Introduction   1
Chapter I: Money, Money, Money   3

Chapter II: Needs vs Wants vs Entitlements   6
Chapter III: Be Innovative, Be Creative   10
Chapter IV: Savings – The More, the Better   13
Chapter V: Spending the Fun Way   17
Chapter VI: Debt Is Not Always Your Friend   20
Chapter VII: Giving and Helping Others   23
Chapter VIII   Work Ethics Can Make or Break You   25
Chapter IV: Have a Plan, Set Goals, Budget and
                        Stay the Course   29
Conclusion   32
Sample Budget   35
References/Sources   37

For I know the plans I have for you, says the Lord, plans to prosper you and not to harm you, plans to give you hope and a future.

Jeremiah 29:11

INTRODUCTION
Train up a child in the way he/she should go, and when he/she is old he/she will not depart from it.
Proverbs 22:6

My mother would always tell me that "Money does not grow on trees". As a young child, I did not know what she meant. However, I quickly learned when I did not get what I wanted after pleading and begging about why I had to have "it".

Do children care about finances? Do they care where the money comes from? NO!! All they want is their stuff: toys, clothes, having fun, and the latest and greatest electronic gadgets. Things that make them feel good. Let's not forget about the goodies: candy, cookies, and good tasting food.

Children think money grows on trees. Children, especially very young children, need to understand that parents earn money by working, either in the home or outside of the home. They also need to know parents are responsible for providing shelter, feeding, educating, and clothing them. Those other things are wants.

Money: we all need and use it. Children, depending on the age, know it has some meaning. Toddlers and younger children see it as a means to getting stuff, whether it is candy, and other goodies, and/or toys. Children view it as a way of getting what they want when they want it. As they get older, many still see it as a means for getting what they want. If they do not have the money, they believe parents are obligated to use their money to ensure they (the child) are happy. WRONG! We as parents need to introduce the concept of money at an early age. Throughout my adult life, I have seen how toddlers to young adults, have a sense of entitlement and think parents have to buy them whatever they asked for. If they do not get it, the attitude surfaces.

Remember Mommy and Daddy, children observe your behavior and you are the focus of their view on finances. Parents, whether you realize it or not, you are constantly teaching your children about money management. They observe your shopping habits, how you put money into savings, and if you are spending responsibly or not. As parents, we must set a good example. I firmly believe that teaching children about money at an early age will minimize a lot of the headaches parents face and help our future adults become good money managers. This book will not go into investments, the stock market or anything like that. It provides real life situations and offers basic money management tips that will help adults teach children to navigate through money challenges they may face in their future.

As parents it is our responsibility to teach our children what they need to know about money to include spending wisely, saving and safe ways to invest.

CHAPTER I
Money, Money, Money

I learned about money at an early age. When my brother and I were in elementary school, my mother took us to the bank, had the bank representative speak to us, and we opened up our first savings account. When we got our allowance for doing our chores, half automatically went into our savings account. We were taught the concept of planning and saving for the future. Our needs were taken care of by our parents. Our wants (goodies and other fun stuff) were our responsibility. The portion on our allowance that we kept was spent on what we wanted, within limits. If there was something that we wanted and did not have the money for, the negotiations began. The outcome was save your portion of the allowance for buying your wants or wait for your birthday or Christmas if you wanted Ma or Dad to get it. Money in the bank was there for a purpose – a long term goal.

What is Money? It is valuable, useful, light, easy to carry, and can be broken into smaller units for easy exchange. It serves as a medium of exchange for goods and services. It is used every day of our lives.

What is currency? It is the type of money used in a particular country such as the United States. Currency in the United States is in the form of dollars and cents/coins. It comes in a number of denominations such as $1, $5, $10, $20, $50, and $100. The coins consist of pennies, nickels, dimes, quarters, and half-dollars.

What is money used for? Money is used to spend, save, invest and give away. In many cases, money is earned either by working or accomplishing a milestone. What you do with it when you get it, will determine how well you can manage it. Learning what money is and what it is used for is essential to good money management.

How do we get money? We get money several different ways.
   a) By working – whether it is for an employer or being self-employed (working for our self).
   b) Monetary gifts – money given for birthdays, graduations, losing a tooth (small children call tooth fairy), or other memorable events.
   c) Allowance - an amount of money that parents give to their child after completing a task, chores, or whatever is agreed upon.
   d) Chores - a routine task or job; a specific piece of work required to be done as a duty or for a specific fee.
      - Allowance tips:
         1) Be consistent when giving out an allowance.
         2) Set limits on how much your child will get.
         3) Set a regular pay day schedule (weekly, biweekly, monthly).
         4) Have a chart or some type of written document with what the allowance will cover.   Make it clear the chores or tasks outside of the written document is required to be done and allowance will not be given for things such as studying and getting good grades. In my family, school was my children's unpaid job. The benefits of doing well in school were it gets the child to the next level in life and their future career. For chores or tasks not completed, money will be reduced or not given.
         5) A percentage of allowance automatically goes into savings for long term goal/purpose.
         6) Monitor what they spend their money on. Let them know that items that are inappropriate are a "no".
         7) A percentage goes to charity/tithes.
         8) Make up a budget for the child – how much they get, what goes into savings, what **goes to** charity, what is spent, and what is left. If money is

left such as coins, small bills discuss putting the money in a piggy bank. You will be surprise how much small change can add up.

CHAPTER II
Needs vs Wants vs Entitlements
Spending in a Good Way

Rae's Story

My children and I often went shopping together and on several occasions, my daughter would see something she really liked and wanted me to buy. She would go into her performance. She would take the item off of the rack or shelf and start her appeal, "This is really nice, don't you think it is Ma? Look at it, this really would look good on me. See Ma. I wish I could get it." She would walk around the store with the item, holding it up in full view of wherever I was, making sure she had my attention. Her dialogue continued, "I could wear this to school and church. This will go well with some of the things I already have. It is on sale and it does not cost much. This is very affordable, Ma. I really like it". This dialogue would go on until I finally would tell her "No, I am not going to buy it." I told her on a number of occasions, that there are other things more important that she needed.

She continued, "Please Ma, I need this. I will pay you back. It does not cost that much, see." I would proceed to walk away and tell both children that it was time to go. I started getting used to her performances.

Children are funny. The tactics they use to get parents to buy stuff is amazing and in some cases creative. Commercials and ads are good at enticing them. They are designed to get the children's attention, not the parent. Helping children understand the difference between needs, wants and entitlement is important. Just because they see something they want, does not mean they are supposed to get it.

What is a need? A need is a lack or shortage that causes a clear adverse outcome. It is something required for a safe, stable and healthy life (e.g. food, water, home). Needs are food, shelter, clothing, and education; the necessities in life. Some may think education is not one of the necessities. I disagree.

    a)   Our bodies need food (vegetables, fruit, water, and meat) to survive.
    b)   Clothing is essential for covering our bodies.
    c)   Housing/home is a place to live and it keeps us out of the natural elements (snow, wind, sun).
    d)   Education is a process by which knowledge, characters and behavior of the human being is shaped and molded. It involves teaching us reading, writing, and mathematics. It is needed to prepare us for daily living and the future (employment).

What is a want? A want as a desire or a wish for something. It is something we might like to have such as toys and entertainment rather than a requirement for healthy living.

What is entitlement? Entitlement is the feeling that you have the right to do something or the right to have something without having to work for it or deserve it, just because of who you are.

Tips:
    a) Teaching children the difference between needs, wants, and entitlements helps them have a better understanding of what is important in life.
    b) Give examples of needs, wants and entitlement. Explain to them that needs will always be the first priority to their wants. So when children say "I need that." It is okay to say "No." The child may want that toy or gadget right now but if groceries, school clothes, or some other need is priority, the need always comes first.
    c) When children understand that you are not

obligated to buy them everything they want and that they are not entitled to the wants, it builds character and an appreciation for those "wants" when they get them.

Stephon's story - Jordan's or not

About 4 years ago, I was taking my godson, Stephon, home one day and he explained to me that he needed the latest pair of Michael Jordan tennis shoes. I asked him why, how much did they cost, and who was going to buy them. He stated that he needed them for school, that they cost about $200, and that his mother was going to buy them. I asked him how much money did he have, and was he going to help towards the purchase of the tennis shoes. He said he had about $25.00 and whatever was in the saving account he and I opened together. News flash. The agreement was the money in the savings account was off limits, it's for college.

My next question was "why were you supporting Michael Jordan. Someone who is rich and has money, while you do not have any. Why are you making him wealthier? Is he going to help you with college? Michael Jordan already has money and you don't." I continued with, "Every time you buy his shoes, he kindly says thank you for giving me more money. Unfortunately, he is not going to give any back to help you. Do you realize that his family is doing fine? He is probably paying cash for his children's college tuition."

I asked him what he was doing with the Jordan's that he already had. Where are they? He said they are too small or in the trash. My comment, "$200 wasted. You could have purchased three or four pairs of shoes of good quality for the price you paid for those Jordan's just because of the name on the shoes." As the conversation continued, I told him to "Stop making Michael Jordan richer. Unless he is going to give you some of that money back, stop giving him more money.

My godson felt he was entitled to a pair of Michael Jordan tennis shoes. Recently he informed me that he has not purchased a pair of Jordan tennis shoes in several years. Hallelujah, he got the message. I am not saying that he will not buy Jordan's again, however he decided to put his priorities in order.

My goddaughter, Ahleena reflected back on her childhood. She told me that as a child her family was not rich, though they still made a way to get what they needed. She went on to say, that if she wanted something that she knew they could not afford, she would ask a certain parent. Her father primarily would buy her and her sister what they wanted. However when asking her mother for something such as a toy, her mother would explain to that they could not afford to pay for it. Ahleena therefore would use the only method that she knew would work - choose the right parent when it comes to finances and getting what she wanted. Ahleena is now an adult and understands the difference between a need versus a want. She can no longer play her parents against each other anymore.

TIPS:
   a) The need is the priority. The wants are likes and children are not entitled to receive the likes.
   b) Have children write their wants in the order of importance. This helps them with planning and organizational skills.

CHAPTER III
Be Innovative, Be Creative
God gives all of us talents, we just have to tap into them

Joe's Story

One day my son came home from school and informed me that he needed a new pair of tennis shoes. He was very specific. They had to be Reeboks. That was the most popular name brand at that time. He was about 7 or 8 years old. It was in the beginning of the school year and he had just gotten a new pair of tennis shoes for the start of the school year. I listened and explained to him that he had just gotten a new pair of shoes and I was not going to pay $75-$90 for a pair of Reeboks. He pleaded and continued to explain how he was the only person in his school that did not have Reeboks and he had to have them. The conversation ended with me telling him that, "I guess he will be the only person in school without Reeboks because I was not buying them."

Several days later, I went into his room and noticed something on his new tennis shoes. To my surprise, he had very neatly took a black marker and wrote Reebok on the back of each shoe. He did a great job. My son proudly wore his new makeshift Reeboks every day. Apparently, they were a hit because he never came home complaining about how someone did not liked his new Reeboks. Innovation is awesome.

Rae's story 2

I observed my daughter as she became a self-taught graphic artist. She has been making birthday cards, flyers, and posters since about age 8. I was in a woman's group several years ago. Every quarter the group celebrated all the birthdays in that quarter. My daughter volunteered to make cards for each lady who was celebrating a birthday. She personalized each card to include their name, birthday date and a personal birthday note exclusive to the birthday recipient.   She made 25 birthday cards. The women loved the birthday cards and were so touched by their own personal card. The director of the group wanted her to make other cards for the next group. She now designs t-shirts, wedding invitations and other crafted items. My daughter is in the process of turning her creative juices into a business.

My daughter and goddaughter, Autumn designed the cover of my first book, "Laughing to Keep From Crying, This Alzheimer's Thing is No Joke". My goddaughter is a natural artist and has been drawing ever since she figured out how to hold a pencil. She is now in college and recently had her own solo art show at her college, displaying her art pieces.

Other examples

My friend's daughter, Hannah was seven years old when she would often attend homeowner association meetings along with her mother. As a result, she felt comfortable talking to adults in the community. One hot summer day, she along with five other little girls decided to wash cars to make money. Hannah would talk to the adults and establish a price from $10 - $20. She had an agreement with the five girls to take $2.00 per car for herself. While the other five girls worked, Hannah brokered the deal, located the water source, and retrieved the payment from the neighbours. Hannah's innovative leadership incorporated a relationship with the community and a management perspective to earn $14 for negotiating and organizing the community car wash venture.

Years later as a 15 year old, Hannah was faced with four weeks without an allowance due to being on punishment. She quickly established a cupcake business using cake mix and fresh fruit from her home. She provided free cupcakes to teachers and charged hungry students $1-$2 for a breakfast bite. In the end, she earned enough money to cover her lost allowance.

Tips:

Both of my children's artistic talents have amazed me. What does this have to do with money? A lot. These talents may result into young entrepreneurs, which result into money earned. Money earned requires money management skills.

Children are very creative and can lead. Encourage their creative juices and talents. Fuel their natural leadership skills and abilities. Your child's creativity, innovative juices, leadership skills and abilities may result in a profitable venture. There is no telling what type of profits your child's entrepreneur spirit may turn into overtime.

CHAPTER IV
Savings – The More, the Better
Saving for a purpose

There is a story in the bible called "The Parable of the Talents" Matthew 24:14-29. It talks about a lord (ruler) who gave three of his servant's talents (money): first received 5 talents, second – 2 talents, and third – 1 talent. The first two servants invested their talents and as a result doubled their talents which included interest. However, the third servant buried his talent in the ground for safekeeping. The first two servants were rewarded by their ruler for doubling their investing. The third servant was reprimanded for not depositing the talents with the bankers which resulted in him not receiving interest. The ruler took his talent and gave it to one of the other servants. He was left with nothing.

Several years ago, I hired my godson for the summer to cut and edge up the lawn. One day after paying him, we talked about saving money for the future. I asked his mom if it was okay that he open up a saving account at a local credit union and that I am listed on the account. She agreed. We went to the bank, the credit union representative spoke to him about banking and savings, and he made his first deposit. We talked about goals and I asked him to decide what this account would be used for. He decided that the money will be saved for college (good decision). He was in the 8th grade at the time the account was opened. He recently graduated from high school and his saving account is growing. He has a part-time job, starting college and is still putting money into that account. He recently opened his checking account and decided the money will be saved to buy a car. He is listening.

What is saving? Setting money aside for the future. You can save for short and/or long term goals. In banking, savings refers to savings accounts, which are short-term, interest-bearing deposits with a bank or other financial institution.

What is a bank? A place where something is held for availability; an establishment for the custody, loan, exchange, or issue of money, for the extension of credit, and for facilitating the transmission of funds.

A savings account is a bank account where you can store money you don't need right away but still keep it easily accessible. Saving accounts earn interest on the money that is in the account.

A checking account is a bank account that allows easy access to your money. In most cases, the money in the checking account is used to pay bills and make financial transactions. Therefore, the money may not remain in the account for long. With a checking account, the account holder can access the money by visiting the bank, writing a check, setting up an automatic transfer or using a debit card.

Teaching children how to save is a must.
a) Work with them on setting financial goals. Ask them to think of two reasons they want to save. As one goal is reached, add another. This will ensure they continue to set financial goals.
b) Be creative. Children can make their own piggy banks by decorating coffee or other containers with their favorite images. Explain to the child what the piggy bank is for and why they are putting money into the bank.
c) Label the decorative bank
   1) Coins or if you want to separate the coins have two banks
     a. one for pennies
     b. the other for silver coins
   2) Dollar bills

Note: Coins and dollar bills can be in the same piggy bank. That's a discussion you and the child should have. Let the child decide.

d) When the decorative piggy bank is full, take a trip to the bank for a deposit.

e) Have the bank representative speak to your child about saving for a purpose.

f) Open up a bank account in both of your names (child primary) and let your child deposit the money.

Taking children to the bank with you and allowing them to observe you conduct banking transactions, shows them the importance of saving. Saving for a specific goal helps children understand the value of money and the concept of saving for a purpose. There is a difference between saving money generally and saving for the future. Teach saving for the future. Whether your children use a piggy bank, envelopes labeled savings to put dollar bills, and/or putting money into the bank account, what matters is getting your child in the habit of saving for the future.

Note: The saving account is their account, not yours to take out money when you are short. Money should not be touched. Even after the goal or purpose is met, have your child come up with another goal and continue to put money into the account for the future.

My mother would also tell me to save for a rainy day. That "rainy day" is the goal. You also want your children to know that when they put their money in a saving account, the bank actually pays them. Wow! Look at their faces and watch the excitement. When they get their bank statement, show them the interest that the bank gave them. No matter how small the amount of interest, explain that the amount is more money that they had before and the more money they put in the savings account, the more interest they will earn.

One of my friends told me how she started a savings account when she got her first job. She decided to set up an automatic withdrawal of $25 each time she got paid. No matter what happened and how many times she changed jobs, she would always ensure that the $25 automatic withdrawal continued. She retired from her job recently. Can you imagine how much money, including interest that account accumulated for the past 30 plus years? Suppose your child starts a saving account now and does not touch it until they retire from their job 30 plus years from now. Guess what, it is not too late for you, parent, to start a separate savings account and have an automatic withdrawal for $10, $20, $25 or whatever you choose. It does not matter how much, just start to save and do not touch it.

CHAPTER V
Spending the Fun Way

When I was in college I got an internship in a department store as an assistant buyer for the china department. It was an eye opening experience. I learned what stores really pay for items. The mark up can be over 200%+ in a lot of cases. What you pay in the stores is far more than what the store pays for the item. Example: You may pay $50.00 for item. The store may pay about $3 - $5 for the item. After that experience, I decided that I would shop around and not pay full price for items especially designer/high end items.

Children can understand the basics of comparison shopping. So… show them how to compare brands to save money. When your child wants to buy something with their money, show them how to comparison shop. Together, go online to the store's website or view the stores sales circulars and show the child the different prices – original and the sale price. This helps them learn to get the most out of their money.

Tips:
When you go shopping, let the child help you make a shopping list. Find a sales paper from the grocery store or where ever you are going to shop and go through the list with them. Find items that your family needs. Ask them to find the sale item. Make it a game. Explain to them the "sales items" mean the item cost less than the original price and you are saving money by buying it for less.

   a) Television, commercials and other ads are designed to entice children and parents. We must have the latest and greatest items, no matter what the cost. When children see these items, the pleading and begging comes and we as parents try to do everything possible to get the items. Many times when we do not have the money to make the purchase - out comes the credit cards, which equals debt. We will talk about that later. Have a discussion with children about the things they see on television commercials and other ads.

b) Help children to think, plan, budget and make sound and wise financial decisions, especially when it comes to spending. My godson realizes that college is more important than making Michael Jordan richer. Always research ways to find the designer items at discount prices. I purchased a pair of tennis shoes at the thrift store for $10.00. They looked brand new, not a scratch or scuff on them. When I got them home, I noticed that they were designed by Michael Kors. The original cost was $150. Look at God.

c) Teach them about comparing the price of what is listed on those commercial ads and things that are similar/good quality and less expensive. Search for the best buy.

d) Teach them how to budget.

A friend of mine told me of an incident involving her son when he was a teenager. He had just received his first paycheck and wanted to go shopping. He wanted to buy a pair of tennis shoes, a cassette tape (music), and some other items. After purchasing one of the items he wanted, he realized he did not have enough money to make the other purchases. He look to his mother and asked her if she could give him $10 so that he could make a purchase. My friend stated that she told her son "you will have to wait for your next paycheck to make the remaining purchases". Needless to say, her son was **upset. He called his grandmother and told her that his mother would not give him the rest of the money to buy his other items. His grandmother informed him to start saving half from this check and add the difference with his next pay check to make his wanted purchase(s).**

The above story teaches several tips.

a) Explain to children that it pays to live within your means.

b) Explain to children that wants are not needs. My friend's son had to understand that none of the items were needs, they were wants.
c) Teach children not to spend more than what they have. Always have a cushion. Teach your children to limit their spending and spend less than what they have instead of more.
d) Teach children to have a plan and save extra money for your wants.
e) Children need to understand that when the money runs out, the spending ends. Teach your child once they purchase what they want and they run out of money, that's it. You, the parent should not always bail them out by giving them the money to buy their wants.
f) Teach children not to spend all their money at one time just because they have it. My mother use to tell me "Not to put all your eggs in one basket." That meant several things." However in this case it means don't spend all your money at once and in one place. Shop around.

My goddaughter, Autumn, likes shopping at thrift stores. She is great at finding items that are unique and making them stand out when she wears them. When she was in high school, she participated in a college bound program at Howard University. One day she wore at particular item and her class mates asked her where she got it. Autumn told them that she bought it from the "Village". They wanted to know what the phone number or website was to the "Village". Little did they know, she was actually referring to Value Village, the thrift store.

CHAPTER VI
Debt Is Not Always Your Friend

My brother took my daughter and her best friend Christmas shopping one year. The girls were about 6 years old at the time. According to my brother, while they were in the store, my daughter's friend found something that she wanted to buy her mother for Christmas. When they got to the counter, my daughter's friend proceeded to take out a credit card. The credit card was one of those fake cards that banks send potential customers when they want to extend credit and get you in debt. The store clerk obviously could not accept the credit card. My daughter's friend told the clerk. "That's how my Mommy pays." Obviously, my daughter's friend was not able to buy the item.

What is debt? Debt is a deferred payment, or series of payments that is owed in the future, which is what differentiates it from an immediate purchase.

What is credit? The ability of a customer to obtain goods or services before payment, based on the trust that payment will be made in the future.

Debit Card versus Credit Card – What is the difference?

What Is a Debit Card? Debit cards are similar to credit cards however there is a difference. Debit cards are issued by a bank or credit union and linked directly to your checking account when you make the purchase. They do this by placing a hold on the amount of the purchase. The store or service provider sends the transaction to the bank and it is transferred to the merchant's account. Once the transfer is approved the transaction goes through. If there is not enough money in the account, the transaction will not go through. It's important to maintain a balance in your checking account to make sure you do not overdraw your account.

What Is a Credit Card? Credit cards are also issued by a bank to people (cardholders) to pay for things or services without paying for the purchase up front. The cardholder promises to pay back the amount(s) borrowed on the credit card. If the total amount is not paid back in 30 days, there can be a cost to borrowing that money known as interest and fees. Credit cards have limits on the amount the cardholder can borrow. Most credit cards have high interest rates, and your credit card balance and payment history can affect your credit score. Credit cards are not always your friend.

Charge cards are also similar to credit cards. The difference is they are issued by retail stores. However they follow the same guidelines as credit cards.

Tips:
   a) Talk to your child about debit cards, credit cards, and charge cards. Explain the pros and cons about the use of each type of card.
   b) Explain to your child that when a credit card is used, it is not their money, it is not free money, and the money belongs to the bank. When the credit card is used, the money must be paid back. If it is not, the bank will charge interest.
   c) Experiment with your child about borrowing. Let them borrow some money from you for a period of time. Provide stipulations on when payment is due. Example: Loan your child $10.00 with the promise that the amount must be paid back in 30 days. If it is not paid back, you will charge them interest/penalty fee – 21% ($2.10) for each month the balance is not paid back. Make sure you put this agreement in writing and the both of you sign the agreement. Even though this is an example, your child needs to know that banks do not give breaks. The interest charge will continue every month until the amount is paid. Missed payments

can result in bad report to the credit bureau, phone calls, delinquent letters and ultimately you being sued.

Note: Parents never co-sign for a credit, debit and/or charge card or any other loan with your children. If payment is not made, you are responsible for the payment.

d) Make it clear to them that under no circumstances, they should never let anyone use their credit or debit card and be pushed into buying items for friends/family.

e) Teach them never charge more than they can pay back.

f) Encourage your child to pay for purchases with cash and to avoid debt monster. Do not be depended on the credit card or buy frivolous purchases. Share and be open with them about your debt challenges and struggles. Being open with them about what you have gone through with indebtedness will help them make wise decisions and practice being debt-free versus debt-bondage.

Due to the type of career that I had, I saw young adults, fresh out of college, with enormous debt from credit card and other personal loans. They had more debt than income. Society pushes credit card and other debt like going to the store and buying candy. It is so easy for anyone to get credit cards and personal loans nowadays. My children learned this concept early in life. My daughter at one time refused to get a credit card. She only made purchases using her debit card and was careful with that. She made sure she had enough money in her account to pay for the purchase. Both of my children learned to be frugal.

CHAPTER VII
Giving and Helping Others
The Importance of Giving Back

When my children were young, I made sure they were involved with giving back by donating their time and money. Each year we would adopt a family for Christmas and they would go with me to select the gifts for the children and the parent. I made sure they took some of their allowance to purchase at least one gift for the child. We continued giving back as a family well into their teen years. They now are avid givers, not only with money but with their time. Teaching children to think of others instead of themselves is a blessing and virtue. It teaches children that life is not all about them but about the willingness to help someone other then themselves. God instructs us "to do unto others as you would have them do unto you". The true blessing is when we think about and help others.

TIPS:
   a) Talk to children about the importance of giving.
   b) Encourage children to give some of their allowance or other earnings to the less fortunate. Set aside money in a piggy bank (younger children) or put money for charities in an envelope and label it charity.
   c) Talk to your child about what they feel strongly about and help them find ways to give back to help someone else.
   d) Create/research opportunities for children to give back and volunteer. Have them give suggestions on how they want to give monetarily and volunteer their time.
   e) Review a list of charity organizations together and have your child pick one that supports a mission they value.
   f) Volunteer and give as a family. Children observe your behavior. When you give you are instilling the

importance of doing good deeds such as charitable work and giving monetarily.

My son continues to give back to his college with his time. He is an avid recruiter for the college he attended.

My daughter always loved working with children. I learned that first hand. She would befriend the children that was the least popular. I remember when she was about 5 years old, there was a little girl who walked with a severe limp. One day I noticed my daughter walking really strange like something was wrong with her leg. I asked her was her leg hurting and she said "no", that she was walking like that so her friend would not feel bad. As an adult, she continues to gives of her time to help children and young adults by encouraging and instilling in them positive life lessons.

I made sure my children volunteered at nursing homes, various shelters, food pantries and other facilities that needed help from others. They packaged and gave out food baskets, sat and talked with the elderly, helped serve food, collected clothes and gave to various shelters – you name it, they did it. Giving teaches children to be selfless not selfish and to appreciate what they have. My children were also taught about tithing - that 10 percent of their earnings belong to God.

The bottom line teaching children about helping others is vital. This is a great way to teach about sharing, kindness and how money, no matter the amount ($1 or $10) can be used to help someone else. Children should understand that they can also give by volunteering their time as well as giving money. Setting a good example for children by teaching the concept of giving discourages selfishness and greed. As children learn that life is not all about them but about being a blessing to others, they will experience the joy that giving brings to someone else.

CHAPTER VIII
Work Ethics Can Make or Break You

My brother and I started working summer jobs by the time we were fourteen years old. This opportunity provided us with an enhanced sense of responsibility as well as an independent source of income. It also taught us good work ethics. Not only were we introduce to the work force, we also learned how we were to conduct ourselves while we were working. Being respectful, doing the best job possible, going above and beyond that the job requires, and be willing to help others is key to success and good work ethics.

Stephon's Story 2

My godson and I often have great conversations about a number of things. Some of our conversations involve spending matters. As I stated earlier, I hired him to cut my grass during the summer. He was not old enough to get a job and he wanted to buy stuff with his own money. The first year/season, he did a great job. I was getting a lot of comments on how good the lawn looked and I made sure I told him how proud I was of him and about the comments. The next year turned out to be a different story. The routine was the same. His mother would bring him over while I was at work (mid-day). She would open the door with the key she had and leave him to do his job which was cut the grass and edge the yard. When he was finished, he was to come in the house, eat lunch and watch TV and play the PlayStation that I had. Then, I would take him home when I got home from work. He was there for about 3 or 4 hours. I trust my godson.

However, he got a little cocky and lazy. He started the season off fine. Doing exactly what he was supposed to do. Gradually, I noticed him slacking off such as the lawn was not completely finished when I got home or he had not edged up the yard. I spoke to him about my observations and asked him why he is not completing the work he was supposed to do. I also talked to him about the consequences of doing less than satisfactory work. I explained to him that no matter what type of work he was doing (schoolwork or working for someone) he must always do the best job he could do. I spoke to him about the importance of doing the best job when someone hires him to work for them and that slacking on the job and unfinished work was unacceptable. I hired him to complete the work before I got home, and to do it well. If there was an issue, he was to let me know. The last straw was when I came home and again the yard was not completed and he was playing video games and eating. I told him he was fired and explained to him why. I also relayed that information to his mother. He did not get paid because I had to hire someone else to complete the work.

I asked him if he understood and that I still loved him but he could no longer cut my yard. The fall of the same year, the person I hired to work on my yard asked my godson to help him rake the leaves and help clean the yard. The man spoke to him and showed him great work ethics. This was a teaching moment for him. He got paid for the good job he did and saw how hard work does pay off.

I always told my children and godchildren that whatever you do, be the best you can be, with no exceptions.

Good work ethics are critical. Be respectful even when the circumstances are challenging, (e.g. crazy supervisor, difficult co-workers) and always be pleasant. Prayer helps a great deal. Do your job to the fullest. Do not hesitate to ask questions, if you are not sure of what is required.

Reality of a Career

I love my godson. We have good dialogue during our time together. His mother called me one day and asked me to talk to him about his views on what he expects to make when he gets out of college. When my godchildren do not listen to their parents, I am next in line. He explained to me that he felt as soon as he gets out of college, he will be making close to $100,000 a year. So I had to break it down to him. Many college graduates don't make nearly this much once they get out of college.

I gave him my story. When I graduated from college, it took me several months before I got a job. I ended working at a women's clothing store as an assistant manager making about $5.00 per hour. I will never forgot when my supervisor approached me after about 3 months into the job. She was so excited. She had spoken to the District Manager about the great job I was doing and my work ethic. They decided to give me a raise. She said to me "that I am quite sure you noticed a little extra in your paycheck last week." I did not have the heart to tell her that I did not notice. When I got home, I looked at my pay stub. There was a slight increase reflected on my hourly wage. The increase was 25 cent from $5.00 to $5.25. I realized that I did not notice it because "Uncle Sam" felt he needed it more than I did. I told my mother and we both laughed.

I also told him that it took me about 3 years to finally get into my career field. I worked as a clerk-typist, then a secretary and finally landed my career position. I further explained to him that my children Joe and Rae had similar challenges when they graduated from college. Both worked in jobs that were not in their field for up to a year before they landed a career position.

Children think once they graduate from college, they are going to make a big salary, which is not always the case, especially early in their career. What does this have to do with money management? A lot. No matter what the income is, money management is important. Children who learn to live within their means and not to overspend by using credit cards, getting personal loans just because they can, will be able to make wise financial decisions.

CHAPTER IV
Have a Plan, Set Goals, Budget and Stay the Course

Joe's story 2

My son made a bold decision after working in his career job for 5 years. He decided that he wanted to go back to school to pursue his law degree full time. I was a little concerned when he told me his plan and when he did it. I know he was great with saving his money. However I also knew he had bills (rent, utilities, school, food, cell phone, etc.). After discussions with him, he reassured me that he had saved enough to pay for school and maintain for at least a year or so. Then after that he would seek employment. He explained to me that while he was working, he put money aside for school that would cover his entire college tuition. He also moved to a place where the rent was significantly less than what he had initially been paying. Therefore it allowed him to bank at least three- fourths of his paycheck. Currently, he will complete law school a year ahead of his original timeframe. He had a plan.

Teach children how to set goals and have goals that are attainable, realistic and achievable. What is the most important goal? How much does it cost? Goals and plans are important and they change. The key is to have a plan. I would always tell my children to have a plan and I would ask them to explain the plan to me. Even though plans can change, the goal of the plan is that it gives direction and purpose. Things change and they may not go the way we think they should. The focus is what the outcome will be. Take the necessary steps needed to get to the goal. Stay positive no matter what and be committed to save towards that goal.

Teach Budgeting

One year I decided to give my children a life lesson about where the money goes. On two separate occasions, one month I sat with my son and another month with my daughter and I told them you will be paying the bills this month. Initially they looked perplexed. I put all the bills on the table, pulled out my checkbook and showed them my bank statement which showed my salary for the month. I broke down what had to be paid and when (i.e. mortgage, utilities, insurances, etc.).

I had them write out the checks and I signed them. They put the checks along with the bill statement in the envelope and where the stamp went, they put the date the bill would be mailed. I showed them my budget layout and had them subtract the amount from the paycheck and they saw the balance. We talked about the balance. I explained about saving the balance, setting it aside in an emergency fund and a "things happen" fund. An emergency fund is a savings of at least 6 months of your monthly expenses. The "things happen" fund is a saving in the event something out to the blue comes up.

When I had them do this, the reality sunk in. They realized that parents have a lot on their plate. Children do not know the sacrifice it takes to run a household. This can also help them better understand the importance of good money management, bills, saving, and budgeting.

In addition, when my children graduated from college and got a job they had to decide which utility bill they were going to pay (electric, water, telephone/internet). They were also responsible for paying their own cell phone bill. My position on this was they will be out on their own one day and they need to get in the habit on pay bills and paying them on time.

Note: Some parents may not want to go to this extreme. You may want to just have them sit down with you as you pay the bills either online or by check.

TIPS:

a) When your child wants to do or buy something, have a conversation about planning and have them layout a plan.

b) Instill goal setting in your child.

c) Teach children what it means to budget and to lay out a written budget. There are countless examples of budgets. Choose a simple layout they can follow.

d) Encourage your child to stay the course and see their plan through.

Here is a budget challenge you can do with your child.

When your child gets invited to a birthday party, shop for Christmas gifts or other types of events where they want to purchase a gift, give them a budget. Help them shop for the gift with the understanding that they must stay within the budget limit, taxes included. For example, if the budget is $10, then the gift and taxes must not go over the $10 limit.

Conclusion

I was determined that my children will understand the concept of money, savings, planning, and being financial responsible. Therefore when they were age 5 and 8, I enrolled them in a money management course sponsored by the Maryland Parks and Planning Department. It was geared to children from 5 – 12 years. The instructor was great. He engaged the children, had a participatory workshop, and let them ask questions. He spoke to them about banking, savings, having a plan, making wise money decisions, setting goals. My children along with the others learned a lot and the class was fun to them.

Several years later, I enrolled them into an investment class for children at George Mason University in Virginia. That one did not go over to well. They were bored and not actively engaged as they were during the first course.

While they were in college, I had the privilege to participate in the Money Management ministry at my former church. Michelle Singletary, the author of the "The Power to Prosper, 21 Day to Financial Freedom", is the director of this ministry. In between their college breaks, my children came to a few of her sessions with me (one in particular was on a discussion about the financial fast). They read the book and again learned more tips on being financially sound with their money.

Several public schools have instituted a program called "Junior Achievement Finance Pack". This program gives children the opportunity to experience future personal finances first hand. They are taught about careers, banking, saving, good spending habits, taxes, money management, and more. It would be great if all school systems would add this program to their curriculum.

One of the most valuable life skills a parent can teach their child is good money management. Talking to children about handling money at an early age and throughout the time they are in your home is one of the best ways to instill good money management. Your children are watching you. Your money management behaviors are important to how your children see the value of money and how to handle it.

Be a good money manager. Saying "no" to your children is okay. It's okay not to give them everything they ask for. It's okay not to spoil them by buying them stuff. Just because you did not have things that you wanted early in life, is not a reason to shower your children with stuff. Spending time with your children, showing them how much you love them is more important than stuff.

Parents, make a commitment to teach your children good money management skills. A good money manager isn't about how much money you make, it's about how you manage and plan. Managing your money effectively takes pride in watching a small savings account grow substantially over time. Patience is important and leads to financial stability. Let's raise good money managers.

Dollar and Sense

DOLLAR$ AND ENE

A financial investment seminar at the Seat Pleasant Activity Center teaches students the nuts and bolts of investing and saving.

Seminar aims to teach youths how to invest, save

Newspaper article -Teaching children financial sense early. My children at age 8 and 5 (far left).

Sample Budget

Date	Amount Received (Allowance, gifts, etc.)	Amount for Goal	Amount for Tithes/Charity (at least 10% or more)	Amount for Spending on miscellaneous (candy, etc.)
Goal: What I am savings for: __ How much do I needed to save: $_____				

NOTE: Discuss with child percent of how much to save to meet the goal. Example: 70% of goal such as toy; 10% for tithes/charity; 20% for misc. such as candy, etc.

Once a goal is met, have the child set another one.

Goal: What I am savings for: Arts and Craft set How much do I needed to save: $20.00				
Date	Amount Received (Allowance, gifts, etc.)	Amount for Goal	Amount for Tithes/Charity (at least 10% or more)	Amount for Spending on miscellaneous (candy, etc.)
6/9/2019	$ 10.00	$ 7.00	$ 1.00	$ 2.00
7/3/2019	$ 5.00	$ 3.00	$ 0.50	$ 1.50
Total	$ 15.00	$ 10.00	$ 1.50	$ 3.50

NOTE: Discuss with child percent of how much to save to meet the goal. Example: 70% of goal such as toy; 10% for tithes/charity; 20% for misc. such as candy, etc.

Once a goal is met, have the child set another one.

References/Sources

Scripture quotations taken from The Holy Bible, New King James Version Copyright@1982 by Thomas Nelson, Inc.

Spend Well, Live Rich – How to Get What You Want with the Money You Have, Michele Singletary, First Ballantine Book, and December 2004

The Power To Prosper, 21 Days To Financial Freedom, Michele Singletary, Zondervan, 2010

The Kids Guide to Money, Steve Otfinoski, First Scholastic Inc, April 1996

Finance 101 for Kids, Money Lessons Children Cannot Afford to Miss, Walter Audal, Mill City Press, Inc. 2016

The Balance.com

Wikipedia.org

Dictionary.com

www.ingramcontent.com/pod-product-compliance
Lightning Source LLC
Chambersburg PA
CBHW031505210526
45463CB00003B/1088

9 781686 225086